Bring in More Business

Ron Robinson

Copyright © 2026 by Ron Robinson

All rights reserved. No part of this book may be reproduced or transmitted in any form or by any means without written permission from the publisher, except in the case of brief quotations embodied in critical articles and reviews.

First printing, 2026

ISBN 979-8-218-91196-6 (Paperback)

Contents

Introduction v
Keywords..vii

The Foundation 1

Chapter 1   Personal Principles...3
Chapter 2   Define Your Market..9
Chapter 3   Test Your Market...13
Chapter 4   Focus on What Matters 17
Chapter 5   Stay Motivated 21

Compassionate Sales Practices 25

Chapter 6   Your Message...27
Chapter 7   Build Relationships..31
Chapter 8   Listen and Learn 35
Chapter 9   Meet Needs 39
Chapter 10   Address Concerns and Close............................43
Chapter 11   CSP Inventory...49

Introduction

A retired sales manager recently commented, "I got out of sales in 2022. Companies were being bought up and the relationships didn't matter anymore. It is all about price and discounts now by the guys in the big offices." His idea of sales was taking clients on big trips and out to expensive dinners. Many of us who own or run businesses build relationships with tools and talents that bring in more business in today's unpredictability and confusion.

BRING IN MORE BUSINESS, The Workbook to Increase Your Sales in Today's Turbulent Markets, is focused on integrating empathy and understanding throughout the entire sales process. You will travel through the process with Cary Heidesch, who lost his job during the pandemic and chose to start his own business providing data analytic services; Paula Barton, whose husband lost his job, creating a greater need for her to increase family income marketing financial products; others who have used certain sales practices to help their businesses; and my experiences growing my own business. The process engages customers as people with unique needs and concerns. This approach promotes long-term relationships between businesses and customers.

One of the first best things that ever happened to me was my parents refusing to pay for my tuition to the University of North Carolina (UNC). They believed their son would fare much better in a smaller school. So off I went to St. Andrews Presbyterian College in Laurenburg, North Carolina. However, more determined than ever to attend UNC, I jumped at the chance to earn lots of money selling dictionaries door-to-door in the summertime. My first summer gave opportunities to earn enough to pay my own way, and I transferred to UNC. For three summers, I recruited sales crews and traveled the country selling dictionaries. In my second summer, I made the President's Club by selling more than 100 books in a week. Much later in my career, I set a record for the number of home listings achieved in the first three months of my tenure with a real estate agency in Asheville, North Carolina. Those skills, honed by the

Southwestern Company in Nashville, Tennessee, have helped me navigate the ups and downs throughout a long and fulfilling life.

Company leaders tend to promote their top salespeople to manage and grow sales professionals. Many of these sales managers fail because they are not trained to develop and motivate their personnel. Companies hire people to sell products and services based on personality and technical ability and overlook sales ability. We must do better as we face greater disruption in our markets than ever before. If climate disasters are not shutting down clients or our companies, then we encounter recessions and lost revenue or our communities wrestle with lost labor and product supply interruption or technology imposes hardships requiring sales professionals to adapt and continue on. In the year 2020, I faced these disruptions and learned along with many of you.

The contents of this manual come from my experience bringing in business in good times and bad. You will learn how to build a solid foundation for growing your business and enjoy using a sales model based on listening and learning of concerns and needs of customers using empathy and understanding. Many who enjoy the sales profession find that the proven practices in this model bring in business in today's ever-changing and highly diverse marketplace.

Keywords

How to increase sales
How to motivate people to sell
What sales skills work in today's markets
How to bring in business
How to train staff to bring in business
How to keep focused on achieving goals

The Foundation

Preparing to start or grow your business involves five fundamentals for building a foundation on which you can achieve your vision and goals. The fundamentals include keeping uppermost in our minds and hearts why we are about to do what we are going to do. Our values and principles guide us when we form decisions that can last a moment or a lifetime. Getting clear on WHY we do what we do leads to clearer decisions along the way. Being clear about whom we wish to serve, that is, the market, leads to clearer definition of the products or services we wish to offer. Testing our ideas before pouring lots of money (ours, investors, or loan officers) leads to greater comfort as we begin our new journey. Maintaining a clear focus on the goal is mastered only when we track and adapt as we navigate our way toward our goals and vision. And, finally, it is normal and natural for humans to become discouraged, bored, or distracted along the way. Earning rewards for achievements makes the journey more enjoyable and tasks more attainable. These fundamentals guide managers of sales professionals as well those professionals who interact with clients and potential clients every day. They all reach higher levels of success while navigating today's uncertainty!

CHAPTER 1

Personal Principles

I have a choice when I wake up in the morning. I can choose to talk myself down and look at a half-empty cup of coffee or anticipate a great day with a topped-off cup of perfectly blended coffee with whipped cream. I have benefited from counseling and medications for depression and diabetes. I found a partner who complements and strengthens me every day. My wife, Judy, is the reason why I write books and poetry and wake up with a smile. My workouts of biking, running, and hiking help to stimulate ideas for a healthy life and remain competitive with other consulting firms. These lessons built my personal foundation in order to become resilient no matter what comes my way.

Be Honest

It is OK to be human. The weight of the world lifted from my shoulders the day I took the blame for something that was going wrong. Assigned to cover our real estate office one Saturday, I came in late. An agent criticized me. For some reason, the words out of my mouth were, "Yep, my bad and it won't happen again." The feeling of relief was awesome. Basketball players point to themselves when they make an error in a game and say, "My bad."

Work Very Hard

Work to find better-paying jobs. Never be satisfied with what you are earning. Generate extra income and invest the money you earn. I started over again by selling real estate and working for a nonprofit. Making a living was tough, even working part time with FEMA (Federal Emergency Management Agency) to bring in more income. My focus then and now is do the best job possible every day. Sometimes, I wake up in the night with an idea and write it down to be turned into action the following morning, or, upon reflection, deleted. Remaining focused on the goal is hard work.

Stand Tall

Being passive is not an option. After three years of clawing back from losing my job, home, and all my savings, I learned to take care of every penny and to advocate for myself. It taught me how someone feels at their lowest. One of my first jobs when moving to Asheville was with a nonprofit. I earned a small wage and supplemented it with selling real estate. A year later, I met with the executive director and explained how I could help in other areas of the organization. Within a week, I received an assignment to run a program and turn it around. My income nearly tripled. Another company visited our program and was seeking staff. I joined them and increased my income again. Then I found my love, consulting, and improved my income once again. Standing up for myself pulled me out of darkness and into the light.

Increase Income

Saving money, even spare change, leads to opportunities to invest and grow income. Savings led me to invest in an old house. On weekends and evenings, I renovated the house and sold it, doubling my investment. I found another property in bad shape, negotiated hard, and purchased it at a good price. This renovation took over six months and became a source of long-term rental income before I sold it in a hot housing market. Now my savings are invested in the stock market. Market values rise and fall, so keeping cash on hand offers opportunities to purchase stock when values drop. The importance of developing several sources of income became a goal, including property rental, book sales, consulting services, and stock dividends. Your sources of income will be different, and it takes years to generate enough resources to invest and create three or more streams of income. Develop your vision for three or more income streams, and work toward that vision. A vision helps motivate us to work toward a cause and look forward to each day.

Listen and Win

A workshop participant expressed frustration as we discussed showing empathy. His need was to win every argument. To him, showing empathy was agreeing with the other person's point of view. He felt a deep compulsion to win when debating with someone. His face scrunched up as he accepted the notion that others had just as much right to their ideas as he did to his. On reflection, he explained to our class that most of his conflicts were with his wife. And now, he seeks to approach ideas from her point of view. He had a big smile as he shared his experience.

Smell the Roses

Early in my life, I became addicted to work and money and spent more time with clients than my family. Clients knew me better than my wife and children. There was a total failure to set boundaries for time at work and with my family. When the job vanished, I struggled to engage with my wife and children. Now, I take time to enjoy hikes with Judy and our dog and have reconnected with my children. Priorities now include workouts, spending time in the mornings watching birds at our bird feeders, and visiting our children and grandchildren.

Show Respect

When working with a nonprofit, my responsibilities included finding jobs and coaching people with developmental disabilities in work assignments. One of my clients was a young woman with engaging eyes and a winning smile. Her job at a resort was to take soiled sheets and towels to the laundry and stock closets with clean sheets and towels. One day, several golfers gathered with us waiting for the elevator. One of the golfers was staring at my client. To redirect his gaze, I asked, "How are you today?" He gave me a cold look and replied, "What is it to you?" I refrained from saying what I was thinking. As a child, there was much sarcasm in my family. The lesson was that it is not funny making fun of someone to get a laugh. That person may be laughing on the outside but is hurting inside. It is easy to forget these lessons, but we are best served remembering the arrogance of others and the hurt we create in the name of humor.

These lessons come from my heart and experiences growing through life and hard times. Many of these principles keep me positively focused and willing to stand up and fight circumstances that, in the past, would bring me down. Taking time to reflect has become my way to stay in the light and away from the black hole I fell into. Each of us has lessons we have learned, and I wish you the best as you reflect on your life's lessons and the stories I share with you.

Be Honest
Work Very Hard
Stand Tall
Increase Income
Listen and Win
Smell the Roses
Show Respect

Practice

Exercise

List 5 values you have learned thus far in your career.

1. ____
2. ____
3. ____
4. ____
5. ____

CHAPTER 2

Define Your Market

Many entrepreneurs want to save the world and help anyone and everyone. But business doesn't work that way. Having a clearly defined market focus provides the ability to understand the characteristics of that market and to design better marketing and business strategies. The goal is to clearly define your product or service and identify those who will be your customers.

Product/Service

Clarify what you want to sell and who would be your customers. Before Toyota built its first manufacturing plant in the US, it sent a team of engineers to live for two years in California. Their goal was to study the driver preferences and habits of US drivers. After carefully observing driver habits and test driving US-produced automobiles, these engineers returned home and designed a totally new car. Toyota partnered with General Motors in California and produced the Camry, their flagship automobile in the US.

The more narrowly you define your market, the better your business will become. Our niche should arise naturally from our interests and experience. For example, if you spent 10 years with a consulting firm and also experienced years working for a family-owned business, you may start a consulting business that specializes in helping small, family-owned companies solve their inventory problems. Cary practiced data analytics when he was laid off by Men's Wearhouse during the COVID-19 pandemic. He studied commodities trading and chose to use his talents to help farmers. William Styles moved to a new state and chose to start an insurance practice in a totally new market with young parents who participated in sports events. Paula needed to increase her income to provide for her family. She chose to market her products that protect homes and autos to young mothers. On a larger scale, Nvidia's first offerings included graphics processing units (GPUs) designed for gaming and professional graphics applications. The company gained significant recognition with its RIVA series of graphics cards in the late 1990s, laying the foundation for its future success in the GPU market. It now offers ten categories of products. Amazon began selling books online as the first bookseller to use the internet. Every successful business is clear about the products and services to be offered initially with a vision for the future.

Customers

A couple from California moved to a small mountain town in North Carolina. They thought they knew what local citizens would like and opened a small restaurant offering food prepared for customers in Northern California. Their business went out of business within six months. They made assumptions and did not sample or interview locals before opening their restaurant.

When you look at the world from your customers' perspective, you can identify their needs or wants. Demographics was a valuable tool for Toyota and can be for your business as well. How will your product or service be received by various age groups, genders, locations, education, occupations, and income? What are their purchasing preferences from cash to Venmo? The best way to learn is to talk to prospective customers and identify their main concerns. While NVIDIA serves 19 industries, most businesses specialize in a more limited number of markets. Many, like Paula, William, and Cary begin with one market and expand based on market growth and introduction to new markets.

Paula doubled her business when she focused on attending the places frequented by young moms and included life insurance with her discussions on home and auto protection.

William began defining his new insurance market by listing his interests in sports and business associations. He began attending chamber of commerce activities and social gatherings. Additionally, he began getting to know the customers in his book of business. As he learned their needs and issues, he began growing his network of customers and client referrals.

Cary lived in a rural area and dedicated time understanding his most promising market based on "Go with what you know." He interviewed farmers who needed help deciding on crops to produce and bring to new markets. He listened and learned their needs from interviews and listening to their comments in meetings. Cary, having interest in commodity markets, is now helping farmers! When I think of Cary, I remember the saying, "Never, ever give up!"

Narrow Focus

What You Know

Demographics

Sample—Survey

Practice

Exercise

1. What have you done that you know well and that others would
    want?

    ____

2. Describe who will be your customer base (e.g., retired baby
    boomers)?

    ____

3. Be more specific about your customers (e.g., baby boomers in
    Florida with an annual income of $50,000 or more and between
    the ages of 60 and 75).

    ____

4. How will you learn from your target market?

    ____

5. What should you change based on your reflections?

    ____

CHAPTER 3

Test Your Market

You are ready to check out your product or service with your defined market niche. If the California entrepreneur had invited people off the street to sample their food, they may have remained in business for a lot longer. You can survey people who are customers and those who may become customers by asking them to identify unmet needs. You may want to know if they have interest in new products or services you now offer. Social media offers another option to conduct surveys of potential and current customers.

The advantage is your ability to segment your market demographically in order to tailor messages and product offerings. It is easy to get discouraged if response is less than expected, but keep in mind that people may not be aware of their needs until they hear more from you. When you survey, be certain to provide information on both product or service features and the benefits they offer.

1. **Survey.** Cary created visual presentations of his offerings and then asked people in town and around the county about his service and how they might be of benefit. He learned from farm supply providers that he had a potential market with local farmers in the county. He interviewed farmers to learn of their problems and opportunities. Based on their comments, he revised his offerings. Before choosing a title for a book or making final decisions on content, I survey business owners and executives to learn the concerns and obstacles they experience. Your initiative should begin to take shape as your ideas and client's needs merge to create something new. Consider offering a free trial or sample to evaluate customer responses. Begin sales in a small way in order to gain insight into your costs and income.

2. **People express interest.** Farmers smiled when Cary asked about their concerns. Single mothers nodded and confirmed with Paula how comforting it would be to have someone like them supporting their insurance needs, and people who hear about my book go online to query it while I describe how it helps companies achieve greater success.

3. **Your idea can be expanded.** Honey Baked Hams offers three ways to earn revenue (ham sales, cafe menus, and catering services), Paula has four insurance products (home, auto, life, and commercial), and Cary offers market research and market strategy. I offer four practices for companies to become highly resilient.

4. **Evaluate.** Now it's time to evaluate your proposed product or service. Perhaps you'll find that the niche you had in mind fails to meet the needs of clients or is at the wrong price point. That means you have more research to do or need to redesign your offering, move to a different location, simplify the service, or scrap it and move on to the next idea.

These ideas were most helpful to me. In 2001, I lost my consulting job in Atlanta and moved to Western North Carolina. Selling real estate in Asheville taught me about changing markets. Our home in Atlanta had been on the market for several months, and foreclosure was looming. Our realtor was having no success, so I decided to sell it myself. The market shifted from a sellers' market to a buyers' market within days after the attacks of 9/11. So my approach to selling had to shift as well. Because the buyer now determined pricing, we cut the asking process by $100,000 and advertised our home for auction using flyers in shopping centers. My realtor said it would not work. On the day of the auction, a young couple visited in the morning and left without saying a word. Early in the afternoon, they returned and offered $40,000 more than our asking price. We sold just before Wachovia foreclosed on our home. Putting the buyer in charge sold our house in two weeks in a changing market.

So now it's time to implement your idea. For many entrepreneurs, this is the most difficult stage. I was worried about the steps for selling our property; but if we do our homework, entering the market will be a calculated risk filled with excitement and anticipation.

Survey

People Show Interest

Idea Can Be Expanded

Evaluate Potential

Practice

Exercise

1. Identify the demographics of your customer base.

   ____

2. Describe the wants and needs of your demographic groups?

   ____

3. How do clients pay? Can they easily pay you?

   ____

4. How will you survey your market?

   ____

5. What information on features and benefits will you include with your surveys?

   ____

CHAPTER 4

Focus on What Matters

There is the story of Christopher Columbus, who traveled from Spain to the New World. He did not know where he was going. When he arrived, he did not know where he was. When he returned to Spain, he did not know where he had been. In today's world of work, we are better served by having a clear path forward. That path includes having goals and counting and recording our progress toward those goals. It is said that a picture is worth 1000 words, and in business, that picture is created by collecting critical data and depicting data trends on graphs. Let's follow Cary and Paula, who achieved greater success and income.

In our first meeting, Cary and I discussed building a foundation for his first year in business. We discussed having a business plan. I described a balanced plan consisting of the components of a business that lead to greater success. Those include scorecards with goals and tactics for Finance, Operations, Employees, and Customers. We discussed how each might apply to his business. With no hesitation, he described two goals: 1. Acquire 3 – 4 clients and 2. Generate $80,000 in business. Cary's homework was to set goals for weekly calls and begin using his calendar for planning daily and weekly activities. Here is his abbreviated plan:

Finance: Set up a business account at the bank and an online payment system.

Operations: Reorganize office and install sales tracking software.

Employees: Check out needs of partner in am and plan for personal activities in the community.

Customers: Business cards and key chains for recognition. Set up a networking system.

Paula and I discussed the importance of getting our house in order before taking on new challenges and more clients. That involves getting a clear focus on what we want to accomplish and measuring how well we are doing. Paula was clear she wanted to make more money but got much clearer when she set goals. Her overarching goal was to double her income from $40,000 to $80,000 over the next six months. To know how well she was performing, she developed a weekly scorecard measuring her sales for home insurance, auto insurance and life insurance. She also measured her weekly contacts with prospects. She posted her graphs on the wall behind her desk so that she would see them every morning when she started work. She developed a practice of dedicating two mornings a week for scheduling contacts, and each Friday afternoon, before going home, she updated her charts on the wall. She also set time aside each day for taking care of herself, her husband, and her dog with exercise and time for reflection.

Bar Chart

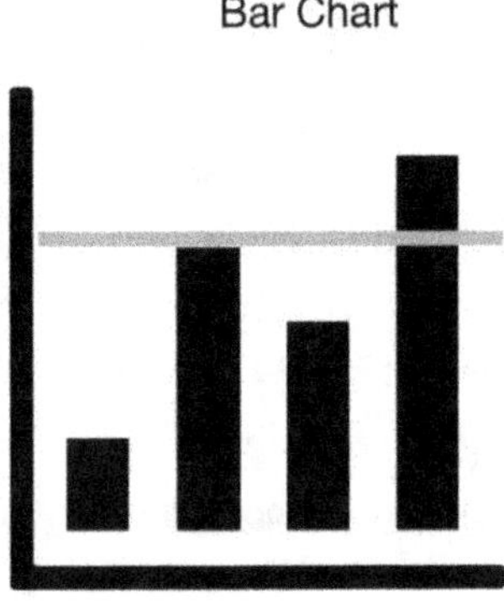

Figure 1. *Bar Graph*

Line Chart

Figure 2 Line Graph

These are two examples of focusing on what matters. The bar graph (Figure 1) tracks weekly sales for each month. The lighter line is the goal, and the dark line is actual sales. The line graph (Figure 2) tracks weekly sales and shows trends. The light line is the goal, and the dark line is actual weekly sales. The reason for tracking data weekly is to be able to adapt early in the month if sales are not tracking to meet monthly goals. Graphing data monthly is easier but useless if the focus is on achieving monthly sales targets. We learn how we have performed only after the month is over, and we lose the ability to change direction during the month.

> Highly Visible Graphs
> Show Weekly Data
> Contain Goals
> Easy to Understand

Practice

Exercise

1. What are your business plans for operating your business efficiently, strengthening your financials, growing customer counts and satisfying employees and family members?

    ____

    ____

2. What are your 12-month goals for your financials, customer growth, organizing your tasks, and taking care of yourself and family?

    ____

3. What are the critical data you will graph weekly to maintain a clear focus on your business?

    ____

4. What are the goals you depict on each graph?

    ____

5. What needs to change for you to gain a clear focus on your business and sales?

    ____

CHAPTER 5

Stay Motivated

Motivation involves how we move toward our goals and achieve them. Research by Dr. B.F. Skinner and others in the field of behavioral science tell us our behavior is a function of consequences and becomes stronger when rewarded and weaker when punished. For example, I will talk longer to someone who smiles at me than to a person who frowns or has a blank expression. We visit people we enjoy being with and avoid others who are grumpy or no fun at all. I discussed with Cary and Paula the importance of rewarding ourselves for achievements in our lives. Cary made plans with his wife for every contact he made and every sale he achieved. He normally washed the dishes after meals. But his wife agreed to wash the dishes when he had a sales contact, and they went out to dinner when he sold a contract.

Paula learned how positive reinforcement can strengthen our resolve and behavior. She planned that for every week she met her goals, she would start the following Monday morning having a cup of coffee at her favorite coffee shop. When she met her monthly goals, she and her husband would celebrate by going to their favorite restaurant. Paula told me that the benefits of these changes were monumental to her success. Work became much more fun, and her charts told her story. She learned from her graphs that her sales came in cycles, not straight lines, and that if she kept her focus and made her calls, her numbers always improved. I offered Paula and Cary three guidelines:

1. **Make it personal.** In other words, make your rewards meaningful to you. If you manage others in sales, be sure to reward their improvements with something that is meaningful to them. For example, a supervisor offered his staff pumpkin bread made by his wife. They loved it and had fun setting goals to get more pumpkin bread!

2. **Make it immediate.** Do not wait to reward improvements or goal accomplishments. Rewards have greater power and influence the closer they are given to personal achievement. Paula's coffee reward was the Monday after her performance the prior week. Cary got relief from washing dishes the same day he met with a prospect.

3. **Make it simple to administer.** A consulting executive kept tickets to ball games and theater performances in his desk drawer. When customers contacted his office to compliment a consultant, he immediately called the consultant into the office and gave them tickets to an event of their choosing.

Cary and Paula learned the importance of preparing to compassionately grow their businesses and wealth by building a strong foundation with the practices just described. In summary, preparing the foundation to bring in business places us in a strong position to expand services and products as we listen and learn from our clients and those around us. We are now prepared to use 5 Compassionate Sales Practices that help me and many others achieve growth and greater resilience in today's uncertain marketplace.

> Personal and Meaningful Rewards
> Reward Immediately after Accomplishment
> Keep Rewards Simple to Administer

Practice

Exercise

1. What motivates you to do the things you do?

   ____

2. How should we reward ourselves?

   ____

3. With whom will you plan to reward your achievements?

   ____

4. What rewards will you use for your short-term and long-term achievements?

   ____

5. What are your plans to stay motivated and goal focused?

   ____

Compassionate Sales Practices

Today's customers are more diverse—five generations and various cultures in most populations—with greater interests and needs to be heard rather than informed and instructed. Social media entertains and solicits input and interaction. Therefore, five practices, known as compassionate sales practices (CSP), in which business representatives use compassion with people offers a competitive advantage for bringing in business. Why the adjective, "compassionate" when addressing how to bring in business? The answer for me is that today's customers expect respect, and using tools of the past can appear aggressive and put off those who may otherwise have interest in what we offer.

The sales talents used for me to sell door-to-door in the 20th century work only in today's markets when modified to build relationships, listen and learn to understand needs, not wants, focus on what helps resolve their needs, satisfy them and close the deal. I was fascinated to experience a client being repelled when I described how to answer objections. She thought that was very pushy. She smiled when I explained that the focus is to learn needs and address concerns. Much more compassionate and the person is now happy using CSP to help others with their needs!

CHAPTER 6

Your Message

A one- or two-sentence message of what your service is and how it helps others is called *The Elevator Talk*. Cary and I worked on his message over several meetings. Here are some pointers I shared as we crafted his message.

1. **Introduction.** Start your pitch by giving your full name, smile, extend your hand for a handshake, and add a pleasantry like, "It's nice to meet you!"

2. **What you do.** Give a brief summary of your background. Include the most relevant information such as your education, work experience, and product or service. If you're not sure what to include, try writing everything that comes to mind on a piece of paper. Synthesize your words to a few points and organize them into two or three sentences that flow and make sense.

3. **Call to action.** You should end your elevator pitch by stating what you want to happen next. Asking for what you want can be intimidating, but it's important that you give the conversation an action item instead of letting it come to a dead end. You have just met this person, so make the ask simple with little required on their part. "I would like to meet with you tomorrow for just 15 minutes. What time works for you?"

If they agree to your request, be sure to thank them for their time and get their contact information. End the conversation with a concise and action-oriented farewell, such as, "Thank you for your time; I'll send you a follow-up email tonight." Cary gave it a try. His first statement was, "I help companies analyze their data." We agreed that was a nonstarter and began refining his message. His next was "I help businesses increase sales by analyzing their data." OK, much better. Clearly, he was getting the idea. As Cary refocused on his clients' successes rather than himself, he created a winner, "I help companies increase sales and donations by analyzing their customer data. The Seattle Seahawks increased season ticket sales and a nonprofit increased donations by $1 million over two years. When can we meet for a few minutes?" The more he practiced, the easier it got to introduce himself at networking events and request meetings. Cary planned to attend a chamber meeting with the goal of obtaining 3 meetings. I could not wait to learn what happened.

<table>
<tr><td>

Introduce Yourself
Tell What You Do
Explain What You Want
Call to Action

</td></tr>
</table>

Practice

Exercise

1. Create your introduction.

   ____

2. Write a brief summary of what you do.

   ____

3. State what you want from the person you are addressing.

   ____

4. Describe your call to action.

   ____

5. Write a one- or two-sentence statement of who you are, what you do, and how others benefit. Try it out with friends to see if they know how you help others.

   ____

   ____

CHAPTER 7

Build Relationships

Building relationships is important for generating business and increasing business opportunities. Building relationships involves finding things in common with your prospect and asking them to set expectations or goals for meetings. Paula and Cary offer stories of how building relations can work for you.

Paula and I met the same morning that I made the ask for a meeting. My first action was to ask her what she would like to cover in our time together. She wanted to know more about how I help others. I asked her to describe her situation and what she wanted to achieve professionally. Her husband recently lost his job, and she wanted to increase her business marketing financial products. We had something in common in that I lost my job when my children were young. I reviewed my book that provides tools and talents for growing a business. Paula agreed we should work together. We set a date for our first coaching session.

When coaching Cary, we practiced building relationships by observing through our zoom screens the objects on our walls and desks with the goal of understanding the other's interests and anything we have in common. I noticed the NC State diploma on his wall and learned of his passion for data analytics and basketball. He observed the trees in the background behind me and noted a totem pole on the back porch. He learned the totem pole represented the consulting services I provided to the Eastern Band of Cherokee Indians. He learned I live on a mountain and graduated from UNC. We learned that we had in common degrees from sister schools, use data in our work, and possess a passion for basketball.

Shannon and Jake, two financial service agents, have just graduated from learning and practicing CSP. In each meeting, I asked what they wanted to learn and to share something that happened recently. In our last meeting, we discussed building relationships. They were startled to be asked to describe what they knew about each other. However, after a bit of prompting, they noted what each had on the walls in their offices and with big smiles noted that one person likes to hunt and that the other has a daughter whom they are very proud of. Jake has no children and Shannon does not hunt. But they know each other better now and are helping each other build their businesses.

By taking time to build relationships with clients, I am able to acquire and grow my business with longer-term work and earning referrals to work with others. Most of my work comes from referrals, as does Paula's, Cary's, William's, Shannon's, and Jake's.

<table>
<tr><td>Find Things in Common
Set Meeting Goals</td></tr>
</table>

Practice

Exercise

1. When in a restaurant or office, look around at the symbols on the walls. What pictures or artifacts do you see, and what do they tell you about the owner?

    ____

    ____

2. The owner of a coffee shop has an office that is poorly lighted, with an old desk and wobbly chair. Papers are scattered over the desktop. What does that tell you about the owner?

    ____

    ____

3. Across the street is a restaurant. It is brightly lit with music, and a person comes out to greet me when I walk in the door. What does that tell you about the owner?

    ____

    ____

4. What would you ask the coffee shop owner to do to build relationships?

    ____

5. What would you ask the restaurant owner to do to build relationships?

    ____

CHAPTER 8

Listen and Learn

Before we can effectively sell our business proposition, we must first learn what our prospect or client truly needs. Much of the time what we want is not necessarily what we need. For example, I may want to take long walks or hikes and sing, but I need to keep the dark walls of depression from closing in on me. So I hike and sing in a church choir to satisfy a critical need of mine. When talking with a prospect I must be aware of their needs. A prospect may not purchase from me if they want to perform better, but they will certainly consider my services if they need to bring in more business to survive and thrive. Paula needed to have enough revenue to cover home and health expenses, and Cary needed to start an enterprise to generate revenue for his family and financial security. That is why it is critical we learn how to Listen and Learn.

Paula and I discussed the difference between wants and needs. Our wants are our preferences, and our needs are our "must haves" in order to conduct our business. As the world famous philosopher and poet Mick Jagger once said, "You can't always get what you want, but if you try sometimes, you just might find, you get what you need." I may want a BMW, but what I need is a 4-wheel drive truck to travel with my dog up and down our steep mountain gravel roads. A client may have wanted his organization to work together but his need was to increase sales and grow his business. To determine needs, Paula and I practiced 3 elements of listening (open questions, rephrasing, and empathy statements).

1. **Open Questions** begin with who, what, why, when, where, and how. For example, you might ask: "What are you proudest of accomplishing with your business? Who is keeping you up at night? Why are your sales below goal? When would you like for those numbers to gain goal status? Where will you find prospects? How will you contact new prospects?" Cary asked his prospect, "How much do you

need to increase your sales? What do you see getting in the way of accomplishing your sales goals?" Paula asked, "What would happen to your home if you or your partner were killed in an accident? What concerns do you have with your current auto and home coverage?"

2. **Rephrasing** involves listening carefully enough to be able to repeat back the essence of what your prospect tells you. For example, Cary might respond by saying something like, "So you wish to increase your sales by 15% but see problems because of lack of personnel." Paula observed, "So you plan home improvements and expect another child in seven months."

3. **Empathy statements** are used to convey an understanding of the feelings your prospect is sharing with you. Communication is not complete unless we know both the facts and feelings being communicated. Basically, people experience four feelings, including joy, fear, anger, and Sorrow. For example:
   - How would you feel if two angry German Shepherd dogs charge at you? Afraid?
   - How would you feel if you toss a ball to play with your dog and he runs away with it? Mad?
   - How would you feel if you toss a ball and your dog returns it? Happy?
   - How would you feel if your pet passes on? Sad?

So let's put it all together. Cary's open questions resulted in learning that his prospect needed to increase sales 15 percent but a labor shortage may slow them down. Cary's response, "Sounds like you have an ambitious goal but may be *frustrated* by not achieving it due to labor supply problems." Cary had a much clearer picture of his prospect's situation by using all three parts of a questioning process to learn their needs and concerns. Paula's summary went something like this, "So you must be *excited* about an addition to your family and getting the house ready! You may feel a *little anxious* about additional costs before long." Your prospect has a much better impression of you for listening carefully to their situation. You have increased the likelihood of earning their business.

Cary and Paula agreed that describing services when beginning conversations was a nonstarter, and both struggled at first with patience and asking questions to build relationships and learn the needs of prospects. Cary's goal was to obtain three commitments for follow-up meetings when presenting to a business networking group. Paula focused on obtaining meetings from her chamber of commerce connections and a women's group.

In our next meeting, I asked Cary, "What is new? How is your wife feeling about your activities?" His good news: he has two appointments this week. We practiced meeting with these prospects. Cary walked through each step using me as his prospect. Starting with relationship, he asked my thoughts about UNC basketball struggles with such talented freshmen. Just like an NC State guy. Then he asked about the UNC loss to NC State, thinking that would build relationships??? He then set a meeting goal using open questions: "What is your goal for our meeting today?" He practiced using questions to identify my needs, such questions being "What data is collected about your customers' buying habits? What data would help you learn more about customer preferences? What do you do with the data you collect? What else would be helpful for you to know?" The secret sauce to learning needs and increasing our business is rephrasing a complete message consisting of facts and feelings.

> Open Questions
> Rephrase
> Empathy Statement

Practice

Exercise

1. What will you ask/observe to build relationships with your prospects?

   ____

2. How will you determine your prospect's goal for the meeting?

   ____

3. Write 3 open questions to ask your next prospect.

   ____

4. Write examples of how clients may experience each of four emotions.

   Joy____
   Fear____
   Anger ____
   Sorrow ____

5. How will you build relationships and learn about prospect's needs and concerns?

   ____

   ____

   ____

CHAPTER 9

Meet Needs

Selling the Sizzle means that you are using persuasion, including **features** that meet the unmet needs of your client and **benefits** that have helped others and that can help your client.

Features are the components of your proposal, product, or service. Features describe what can meet the needs of your client. This is our best part of any discussion at a party, over Thanksgiving dinner, or at a church picnic. We help our friends with insomnia with our lengthy discussions on what we do and how well we do it. For example, I just received a proposal from a book company. Without asking a question, the information described in detail the steps for editing my book, publishing my book, marketing my book on social media, and placing me on the first page of Google searches. This was a clear description of what they can do for me without seeking to learn what I might want or need.

When selling dictionaries door-to-door, I learned that customers may want to know about the book but would buy only if they knew how it would help them. So after describing the tough binding, the completeness of the dictionary with 8 definitions of the letter A and an index in the back, I flipped to the section with pictures and stories to describe how easy it would be for Johnny to write reports using the Bible and History stories. This persuasion model enables many others, including Cary, Paula, and myself to generate business.

Benefits are the WIIFM or What's In It For Me discussion, the Sizzle. For example, "Miss Jones told me that her children were doing much better in school and Johnny is now making B's in English instead of C's! Paula's Sizzle became the story of her client who saved their home and car after a horrible car accident. That Sizzle is why a prospect becomes a customer and buys our products or services. If a prospect does not understand what is in it for them, they have no reason to buy from you or me!

My book company asked my reason for writing my book and what I expected to accomplish. I explained that I want business leaders to possess greater ability to manage their personnel and grow their businesses. I needed the book to have wide distribution in the business community if it was to help my target market. With that information, they reviewed features that could help me, and we settled on our next steps for editing and distribution.

Cary was successful using his elevator talk, writing proposals, and conducting informational sessions when he understood the Sizzle or WIIFM describing how clients benefit from his data analytics. Their eyes opened wide when he excitedly described the results of his services for his clients. Many of Paula's prospects leaned forward as she told stories of how her clients avoided financial ruin during disastrous situations. I reached Presidents Club (100 book sales in a week) when I shared Johnny's success story of rising from a C to B+ English student using Webster New World Dictionary.

Upon listening and learning, Cary and Paula described services that meet unmet needs of their prospects. Watching for head nodding, they learned to avoid overselling. I shared the story of watching a thirty something oversell when making a web design presentation to a business group. The meeting discussions had continued longer than anticipated, leaving only 10 minutes for a 20-minute presentation. Rather than cut the content, he talked faster, describing all the features and benefits of their service as nearly half the members walked out of the meeting. Had this salesperson cut the number of features and adjusted his presentation to 7 minutes, he could have scheduled time to meet members at their businesses. Opportunity was lost by not addressing the needs of his audience. The secret to successful business persons is their ability to listen and diagnose unmet needs and then meet those needs with services and great stories.

<table><tr><td>Describe Features
Tell Stories and Sell Sizzle</td></tr></table>

Practice

Exercise

1. What is your sizzle?

   ____

2. What are your client's needs and concerns?

   ____

3. How do your features solve your client's needs and concerns?

   ____

4. What story can you tell about someone you have helped with those needs and concerns?

   ____

5. What can you change to make your presentation even better?

   ____

CHAPTER 10

Address Concerns and Close

It is my experience that many sales are lost for lack of asking for the business. In stories by Paula, Cary, Shannon, Jake, and in my own experience, we tell our stories and hope prospects will call us. It is human nature for us to avoid putting someone "on the spot" and lose sales we would otherwise have gained. A successful sales professional will ask for the business several times during a meeting to avoid overselling. A gentle close during our presentations can save time and gain more sales.

After a presentation to our chamber of commerce, I made the ask of a person at my table, "I would like to visit with you next week. What works for you?" We scheduled a zoom meeting for later that day. I began the meeting by establishing rapport. My questions were "How long have you been a chamber member? What did you think about the presentation this morning?" My next question sought to understand his goal for the meeting: "What would you like to accomplish with our time today?" "Learning about your services," he responded. After asking him about his business, we were off and running. He described being overwhelmed as a result of restructuring, and I simply said, "It sounds you could use the kind of help I just offered another company that is now thriving. Since it is the end of the day, why don't we meet again tomorrow to better understand how we might work together?" We agreed to meet the following morning.

In our morning meeting, I asked him (JP) to describe his organization and how a day in his life looked. After his description, I offered next steps. "Let's begin by your taking the surveys and getting a book that has helped others like you. Then next week, we will begin a series of classes to help you think through how to best manage your situation. SYX company just overcame similar issues and has just increased their business with the same number of people. How does that sound to you?" Good. "Does next Wednesday or Thursday work best?" Thursday. "Morning or afternoon?" Morning. "What time?" 10:00. Deal closed!!

In this exchange, I asked open questions to learn about him and his needs and tell a story. Closed questions asked for a second meeting. The second close offered choices of days to start and time of day to begin.

I remind Cary of our first meeting. "Cary, when I first met you, I asked you questions that told me you did not know how to sell and needed to be better organized in order to sell. And I learned your goal was to acquire 3–4 clients and generate $80,000 in revenue. Would you agree? Then I described features including a balanced planning model, a compassionate selling model along with practices for selling and closing sales. I told you the story of using those tools and skills to achieved President's Club status in sales and now grow my business. You were asked if you agreed the process would help, and then you were offered choices of days to begin and time of day to get started."

We practiced the persuasion model. He used open questions and occasionally closed. He caught on to the difference between using open questions to learn more about his prospect and closed questions for closing the agreement. We then practiced asking for the sale and offering choices such as "should we begin this week or next," would you rather pay with a debit card or cash?" etc.

Paula and Cary went through practice sessions, keeping in mind the following:

- Listen with several open questions, then summarize and give an empathy statement.
- Present services discussing features that address needs and issues shared with you.
- Sell the sizzle, tell stories of how others have benefited from your services.
- Close by asking two closed questions that elicit a yes answer; give a choice of days to begin working together.

It was now time to discuss fees. When a prospect asks, "How much?" bracket your response. Cary learned to tell how others charge much more and that his is a fair price. For example, "Several firms who offer such a service price their rates between $75 and $300 an hour. The good news is that my service is as good or better and is only $100 per hour!" When hearing concerns about premium costs, Paula began explaining, "Our premiums are lower than several companies' and higher than others'. The reason clients remain with us is because our service is the best and our response team resolves client's issues and gets them paid in days, not weeks or months."

To evaluate Cary's progress, we used a process called Start, Stop, Continue. He listed:

Start: Post a chart in the kitchen listing his daily schedule.
Stop: Checking the news first thing in the morning.
Continue: Practice his presentation and schedule appointments.

We agreed these actions would make business development smoother and more efficient. Our next session was to answer concerns and close the deal. It has been my experience that no matter the nature of the service, prospects have typically 3 concerns.

1. **Money**

    Concern: We are at the end of the budget cycle and money is tight. Or, your prices are high for our company.

    Response: "I understand your concerns about fees and totally agree. That is why I think you are so lucky! You see the fees for my services can be as high as $300/hour. The good news is that because of low overhead, my fees are only $100/hour for services better than what you get for much more, and I guarantee a refund should you be unhappy with my work! When do we begin?"

2. **Time**

    Concern: We are up to our elbows in work now, and it would be very difficult to break our managers loose for the amount of time it would take.

    Response: "It sounds like you are really busy and anxious to get everything in order before much longer. I completely understand. It reminds me of another client I recently served whose company had recently been challenged with daunting goals. They recognized the importance of having the tools and skills offered and had a quick zoom meeting with their management team to create individual schedules for moving forward. So good news, I now have some time to work with your team on different days and times. Would you like to have a quick meeting with everyone tomorrow or on Friday?"

3. **Delay**

Concern: Let me think about it. I will do some research and get back to you. (They are telling you that you have not yet met their needs.)

Response: "Sounds good to me. I am cautious myself when using a contractor. The thing Joe Schmo (use the name of someone or company known by your prospect) liked about my service was it was personal, reasonably priced, and he would have comprehensive data to make marketing decisions. He confessed he wasted too much money on marketing campaigns that did not pay off. He recognized the data analysis I used to help the Seattle Seahawks increase their seasonal sales could help his marketing team make more informed decisions. I know you want your marketing dollars to create more leads, don't you? Let me suggest we meet with your marketing and IT people next week to discuss next steps. What day works best for you?"

Cary began listing concerns he hears and forming messages to resolve those hurdles. The following week, when reviewing his contacts, Cary grinned through his dark beard, and his voice got stronger as he described contacting 3 businesses a day, totaling 21 businesses thus far in the month. Of those 21 businesses, he closed two clients for a 10% close rate. He agreed that more consistent use of persuasion models should improve his close ratio. He set a goal to improve his ratio to an average of one close for every eight contacts, then improve again to one close for every five contacts over the next three months.

My last conversations with Cary and Paula indicated that he is happy and continues to assist farmers create financial models for managing their farms and that Paula achieved her goal of reaching $80,000 of income and earned "agent of the month" recognition.

Money
Time
Delay

Practice

Exercise

1. Analyze why you lost sales (What you **did** or **did not** do).

   ____

2. What is the difference in Listen and Learn questions and Closing questions?

   ____

3. List 3 concerns you hear that get in the way of a sale.

   ____

   ____

   ____

4. Provide answers for each of the three concerns. Begin each answer with "I know what you mean and that is why," or "I completely understand and that is why."

   ____

   ____

   ____

5. How many contacts do you have each week, and how many sales do you achieve? What is your sales/contacts ratio?

   ____

CHAPTER 11

CSP Inventory

1. Message	Who You Are, What You Do
2. Relationships	Rapport and Meeting Goals
3. Listen and Learn	Open Questions, Rephrase, Empathy
4. Address Needs	Features, Stories (Sizzle)
5. Address Concerns	Close, Answer, and Close Again

The following inventory provides a perspective on how well equipped we are to serve in today's turbulent marketplace. Answer based on what you do each day. How prepared are you?

BRING IN MORE BUSINESS	YES	NO
FOUNDATION		
1. YOUR PRINCIPLES		
1. You can describe at least 3 principles you live by		
2. Your principles include family		
3. Your principles include integrity		
4. Your principles include delighting customers		
5. You reflect on your principles when making business decisions		
2. DEFINE YOUR MARKET		
6. You have identified what you do well		
7. You know who your customers will be		
8. You have defined your market based on demographic study		
9. You know what your customers think of your products/services		
10. You know what to change		
3. TEST YOUR MARKET		
11. You know how you will learn from your market		
12. You know what you want to know from your market		
13. You know your market demographics		
14. You have surveyed your market		
15. You have pay systems for customers to easily pay you		

4. FOCUS ON WHAT MATTERS		
16. You have plans for Operations, Finance, Employees, and Customer		
17. You have 12-month business goals		
18. You graph weekly critical business data		
19. Your graphs have goals		
20. You know what to change to achieve a clear focus on your business		
5. STAY MOTIVATED		
21. You know why we do the things we do		
22. You know why rewards are important		
23. You have a plan for rewarding achievements		
24. Your plan will keep you motivated		
25. You involved others in deciding on goals and rewards for achievement		
TOTAL FOUNDATION SCORE		
COMPASSIONATE SALES PRACTICES		
1. MESSAGE		
26. You have created an introduction		
27. You have a written summary of what you do		
28. You ask for meetings when you talk with a prospect		
29. You have a call to action		
30. You can briefly describe what you do and how you help others		
2. RELATIONSHIPS		
31. You can identify symbols that tell you about a prospect or client		
32. You can describe what a dimly lit office says about the prospect		
33. You can describe what a bright office says about your prospect		
34. You are prepared to comment on each situation with a prospect		
35. You begin a conversation by building relationships and setting meeting goals		
3. LISTEN AND LEARN		
36. You listen and learn before telling prospects how you help		
37. You prepare open questions to ask prospects and clients		
38. You express empathy with prospects and customers		
39. You rephrase what you hear before expressing empathy		
40. You enhance relationships when you meet with prospects and customers		
4. MEET NEEDS		
41. You sell the "sizzle"		
42. You describe your customer's concerns		

43. You describe features that resolve client concerns		
44. You tell stories of client successes		
45. You analyze past sales efforts to become even better		
5. ADDRESS CONCERNS AND CLOSE SALES		
46. You use open questions to learn and closed questions to close sales		
47. You can list customer concerns that get in the way of a sale		
48. You have prepared responses to client concerns		
49. You measure your weekly customer contacts and sales		
50. You use the ratio of sales to contacts to evaluate and improve sales performance		
TOTAL CSP SCORE		
TOTAL FOUNDATION AND CSP SCORE		

www.ingramcontent.com/pod-product-compliance
Lightning Source LLC
Chambersburg PA
CBHW050617160726
48003CB00003B/1224